THE NATIONAL TRUST

Investigating
THE VICTORIANS

By Alison Honey
Illustrated by Peter Stevenson

Contents

Published in association with
National and Provincial Building Society

The Empress Queen

When Queen Victoria came to the throne in 1837 the monarchy was in a pretty bad state. Her grandfather, George III, was unwell for much of the time and so his son, the Prince Regent, took charge during the king's illness. He did not set a very good example, spending most of his time drunk, over-eating or being unfaithful to his wife, Princess Caroline of Brunswick (who was not much better than her husband). He ruled as George IV for ten years and when he died in 1830 his younger brother William took over. William was eccentric but not very clever and was nicknamed 'Silly Billy' because his speeches were often rambling and didn't make sense. He didn't have a very good reputation either: he'd lived with an actress for many years and had nine children by her. None of his legitimate children survived childhood, so the heir to the throne was his niece, Victoria, the daughter of the Duke of Kent.

THE PRINCE REGENT

Queen Georgiana?

Victoria's parents had planned for their daughter to be called Georgiana Charlotte Augusta but this was upset by the Prince Regent's behaviour at the christening. He was standing as godfather and, as usual, he was drunk. He took exception to the duke and duchess's choice of names and insisted the baby should be christened Alexandrina Victoria. As a child Victoria was known as 'Drina'.

Diary duty

In her early teens Victoria started keeping a diary which she wrote daily until a few days before her death.

Coronation chaos

Victoria was only eighteen when she came to the throne in 1837 and reigned for the next sixty-three years. She holds the record for being the longest reigning British monarch. However, things didn't bode very well at the start as the coronation ceremony was a complete muddle. The Archbishop of Canterbury put the ring on her wrong finger, so it was much too tight; the altar in the side chapel where the most important people went before processing out of the Abbey, was covered with sandwiches and bottles of wine; and Lord Rolle, an elderly and overweight peer paying homage to his new queen, lived up to his name by repeatedly falling down the steps on the way up to the throne. In the end Victoria couldn't stand it any more and climbed down the steps to meet him.

Monogrammed railings

Victoria's father died when she was eight months old and her mother relied on advice from her own brother Leopold. Leopold had been married to Princess Charlotte, the only legitimate child of George IV, but she had died in childbirth in 1817 after just over a year of marriage. The couple had lived at Claremont in Surrey and Leopold continued to live there until he was made first King of the Belgians in 1831. If you visit Claremont, you can see the railings at the Camellia Garden which were made of a pattern of crowns linked with the letter L for Leopold. Years later, after she became queen, Victoria bought Claremont for her youngest son, who was also called Leopold so his name fitted the railings too!

A smothering mother

The Duchess of Kent was very protective of her daughter. She slept in the same room as Victoria right up until the night before the Coronation. When Victoria moved into Buckingham Palace as queen she made sure her mother had a set of apartments right at the other end of the Palace.

Made in Britain

Victoria married her German cousin Albert of Saxe-Coburg in the Chapel Royal, St James's Palace on 10 February 1840. She was dressed completely in clothes made in Britain.

A quick thinker

Queen Victoria was very sheltered from the squalor of nineteenth-century life and at times could appear very naïve. When visiting Cambridge in 1843 she was walking beside the river with the Master of Trinity College. All the sewage went directly into the River Cam and the water was littered with loo paper. Victoria asked innocently what all the pieces of paper were and the Master quickly replied that they were notices saying that bathing in the river was forbidden! In a sense this was right as no one in their right mind would want to swim in the filthy river.

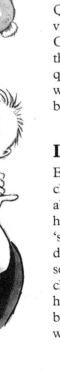

We are not amused!

Put your foot in it

Queen Victoria and Prince Albert visited St Michael's Mount in Cornwall in 1846 during a cruise on the royal yacht. An imprint of the queen's foot was made on the steps where she landed from the royal barge. You can still see it today.

Doting granny?

Even though Victoria had nine children she did not go overboard about young babies and described her fourteenth grandchild as a 'small, red lump'. Her eldest daughter, Vicky, was much more sentimental about the idea of having children but her mother quickly put her in her place, saying that breastfeeding made you feel as if you were a cow!

My beloved Albert

Victoria was married to Albert for nearly twenty-one years and was completely devoted to him. She gradually let him take on more and more responsibility in the running of the country and he had a great influence on her. The queen wanted her husband to have special status, but it wasn't until 1857 that he was given the title of 'Prince Consort'. Albert was a very serious-minded man with high principles and Victoria changed her own lifestyle to please her husband. Before Victoria had met Albert she loved staying up late and dancing past midnight at balls but after they married the couple always left for their supper at eleven o'clock. Much of the serious side of Victorian life is, in fact, due to Albert's influence.

VICTORIA BEFORE SHE MET ALBERT

Family life

Both Victoria and Albert spent a great deal of time with their children and wanted to give them as normal a family life as possible. They spent holidays up in Scotland at Balmoral or at Osborne House on the Isle of Wight which Prince Albert helped to design – it was finished in 1848. Albert took his role very seriously and even directed the planting of the gardens by standing on the tower waving semaphore flags! In 1853 an entire chalet was brought over from Switzerland and put up in the grounds as a playhouse for the royal children.

Like father, like son?

Victoria and Albert's children didn't all inherit their father's serious character. The couple's eldest son, Bertie, the future King Edward VII, was a bit of a rogue. During his long wait to come to the throne he lived life to the full. He had many lovers, ate and drank well, and generally had a good time. He loved hunting and among his more memorable meets was a safari up the Nile, travelling in six steamers carrying 3,000 bottles of champagne, 4,000 bottles of claret, four French chefs and a laundry!

Treading a fine line

Bertie also had an adventurous streak – when he went on a tour of Canada in 1860 he watched a famous tight-rope walker crossing Niagara Falls, pushing a man in a wheelbarrow. For the return trip the acrobat offered him a place in the wheelbarrow which the prince eagerly accepted. His worried advisers – who didn't want to see the heir to the throne plummet to his death – only just managed to persuade him not to get in the barrow!

Laying the blame

When Prince Albert died of typhoid in 1861, Victoria was devastated. A month earlier, Bertie had had an affair with a young actress while stationed with his regiment in Ireland, to the horror of his father. Victoria claimed the shock of hearing of Bertie's behaviour brought on his fatal illness.

One in the eye

Another of Victoria's sons, Arthur, was quite a handful too. He accidentally shot his brother-in-law, Prince Christian, in the eye and doctors had to remove it. Christian seems to have taken it very well and amassed a large collection of glass eyes. He used to enjoy shocking guests at dinner parties by asking the footman to bring in a tray of his favourite eyeballs and swapping eyes. He had glass eyes to suit every occasion – including a bloodshot one which he wore if he had a cold!

A powerful family

Queen Victoria was known as the Grandmother of Europe because so many of her nine children, forty grandchildren and twenty-nine great grandchildren were married to members of European royal families.

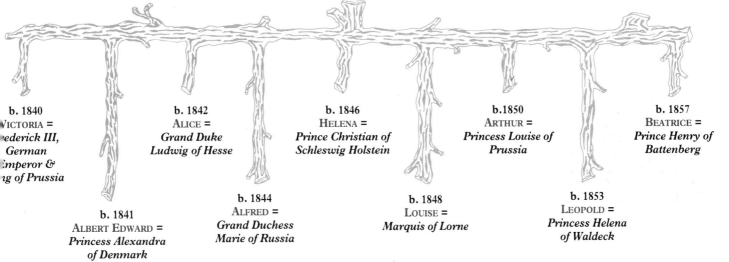

QUEEN VICTORIA = PRINCE ALBERT OF SAXE-COBURG GOTHA

b. 1840
VICTORIA =
Frederick III,
German
Emperor &
King of Prussia

b. 1841
ALBERT EDWARD =
*Princess Alexandra
of Denmark*

b. 1842
ALICE =
*Grand Duke
Ludwig of Hesse*

b. 1844
ALFRED =
*Grand Duchess
Marie of Russia*

b. 1846
HELENA =
*Prince Christian of
Schleswig Holstein*

b. 1848
LOUISE =
Marquis of Lorne

b.1850
ARTHUR =
*Princess Louise of
Prussia*

b. 1853
LEOPOLD =
*Princess Helena
of Waldeck*

b. 1857
BEATRICE =
*Prince Henry of
Battenberg*

End of the world

When Albert died Victoria said 'The world is gone for me'. She wore black for the rest of her life and for many years didn't attend state occasions, spending most of the time as a recluse at Balmoral or Osborne. When she eventually returned to the public's gaze, she refused to wear the crown and robes of state. To many people's annoyance, she insisted on wearing a bonnet for her Golden Jubilee celebrations in 1887!

Wedding blues

Victoria agreed to go to the wedding of Bertie and his beautiful bride, Princess Alexandra of Denmark, in 1863 but couldn't face the reception without Albert and had lunch alone.

Changing times

During her long reign, Victoria worked with a variety of Prime Ministers from the Whig (Liberal) and Tory (Conservative) parties. The queen was often accused of showing favouritism to different Prime Ministers and getting upset when there were changes of government. As a young queen she was very fond of and dependent on her first Prime Minister, Lord Melbourne. Later, her favourite was Benjamin Disraeli, Conservative Prime Minister twice. He was a very flamboyant character and knew exactly how to get round the queen and went some way in getting her to perform a more public role again after Albert's death.

In 1876 Disraeli – or 'Dizzy' as he was nicknamed – passed a bill which made Victoria Empress of India. This meant that she could sign herself Victoria R I (R = Regina (queen) and I = Imperatrice (empress)) instead of just plain Victoria R. Pillar boxes from 1876 onwards showed these initials.

Secret society

Disraeli was a real charmer... He established a club called the Order of the B (B stood for the B of Lord Beaconsfield which he became in 1876) and invited special women friends, including one of Queen Victoria's daughters, Princess Beatrice, to join. Each member was given a brooch in the shape of a bee.

The reluctant messenger

When Disraeli was dying he was asked if he would like a visit from Queen Victoria. He refused, saying: 'She would only ask me to take a message to Albert'. Queen Victoria sent a wreath of primroses, Disraeli's favourite flower, to his funeral. The primrose became a symbol for his own brand of Conservatism, now remembered with the Primrose League.

Gloomy Gladstone

Disraeli's great rival was the Liberal leader William Gladstone whom Victoria really disliked. The feeling was mutual. Gladstone didn't have the knack for treating the Queen right. Disraeli summed up the difference between his own and his rival's approach:

'Gladstone treats the Queen like a public department; I treat her like a woman'.

MR. GLADSTONE

HUGHENDEN MANOR

Flattery gets you everywhere

Another of Disraeli's famous tips on how to treat royalty was this: 'Everyone likes flattery and when you come to royalty, you should lay it on with a trowel'.

Dizzy's home

You can visit Hughenden Manor in Buckinghamshire which was Disraeli's home from 1848 until 1881. Here you will see many portraits and photographs of characters from Victorian times. You can also go to the church nearby to see the monument which Queen Victoria erected in honour of her favourite Prime Minister.

An industrious nation

The greatest exhibition

For six months of 1851 London was the host to one of Prince Albert's brainwaves – the Great Exhibition. A huge temporary building of glass and iron called 'the Crystal Palace' was built in Hyde Park to display the 'Works and Industry of all Nations' – although most of the exhibitors were British manufacturers showing off their goods. There were more than 100,000 exhibits ranging from stained glass to stuffed cats. Thanks to the spread of the railway, more than six million people from all over the country had visited the Exhibition by the time it closed.

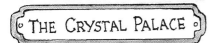

THE CRYSTAL PALACE

An 'enginious' idea

Cornwall had an important tin mining industry which had existed for centuries. However there was a major problem – the deep mine shafts kept flooding which was very dangerous to the miners and disrupted work. In the early 1800s a Cornish engineer, Richard Trevithick, perfected a high-pressure steam engine which revolutionised the way the shafts could be drained by sucking up water like filling a giant fountain pen. It could pump 2,052 litres of water a minute from a depth of 510 metres. Trevithick left England in 1816 to give his expertise to the silver mines of Peru, but his invention meant that Cornwall held the lead in tin mining for most of the nineteenth century.

You can visit these mines at Levant in Cornwall, and see the oldest beam engine in Cornwall working under steam power.

ENGINE HOUSE, EAST POOL, CORNWALL.

The new rich

The growth in British industry and manufacture meant a new route to riches for many people. Some of the new Victorian country houses were built with money made from strange trades like bird droppings (used for fertilizer), biscuit making or even ostrich feathers (used as fashion accessories)!

World leader

During the nineteenth century, Britain became known as the workshop of the world, especially for its great and varied industrial production. In 1870 Britain made more than a third of the world's manufactured goods. By 1900 seventy five per cent of the world's steamships were built in Britain.

Trams, trains and tubes

Transport underwent enormous changes during Victoria's reign. The development of steam trains and boats, trams, underground trains, motorcars and even the humble bicycle revolutionised the speed at which people could travel around and out of the country. When Victoria was a child, the only two options for land travel were by horse or your own two feet – even for a princess.

Firsts in British transport

● The first public railway with steam locomotives was opened in 1825 and joined Stockton and Darlington in County Durham. It was 14 kilometres long.

● The first Great Western Railway train opened to the public left Paddington station on 4 June 1838. It travelled at of 33mph (53kph).

● The first underground line to open in London was the Metropolitan in 1863.

● Horsedrawn trams were used for the first time in 1861. They were gradually replaced by electric trams which came on the rails from 1890.

● The first steamship to cross the Atlantic was *S.S. Great Britain* designed by Isambard Kingdom Brunel in 1843.

Stephenson's Rocket

In 1829 George Stephenson built the *Rocket* – the most famous early locomotive. This great inventor was born at Wylam in Northumberland in 1781 and you can visit his tiny one-room birthplace there.

A growing network

In 1843 there were about 3,200 kilometres of railway in Britain; five years later it had more than doubled to 8,000 kilometres and by the end of the century Britain's railway network covered 29,000 kilometres of track.

The railway museum at Penrhyn Castle, Gwynedd, contains information about these first railways.

Danger, men at work!

Railway construction work was dangerous and workers got paid twice as much as normal labourers because of the use of dynamite for blasting cuttings and tunnels.

Steely grin

Tunnels were not only dangerous to build but could prove hazardous for passengers. A handbook for train passengers recommended men to watch out for pickpockets and suggested that women put pins in their mouths to ward off anyone trying to kiss them in the darkness of the tunnel!

Knock-on effects

The railways took over from canal transport, the main way of moving heavy goods until then. Posting inns disappeared on main roads and post was carried by train rather than mail coach.

Activity Box (Answers on page 32).

Match these carriages to their passengers.

A.

B.

C.

D.

1.

2.

3.

4.

You can see another good carriage collection at Arlington Court in Devon.

Country and carriage

Although railways were spreading throughout Britain, people still needed horse-drawn carriages to travel where there were no railways, to get to the station, or just for daily use. If you visit Calke Abbey in Derbyshire you can see a wonderful collection of Victorian carriages which were used at the house right up until 1924 even though the motor car had then hit England with a vengeance. The reason for this was that Sir Vauncey Harpur Crewe who owned Calke from 1886 to 1924 was a bit of a recluse and banned all motor traffic from the grounds. Anyone visiting Calke had to leave their car at the main gate and be collected by carriage which would arrive with rugs and refreshments to take them the rest of the 3 kilometres to the house.

Just as we have saloon cars, four-wheel drives, open top sports cars and family minibuses there was the same range in carriage design. Some of the types available were broughams, phaetons, governesses carts, landaus, hansom cabs and even dog carts.

HORSE BUS

Did you know?

The word 'coach' comes from Kocs, a Hungarian village famous for carriage-making.

9

Brrrm, brrrm

In 1863 Lenoir, a Belgian, invented the motor car with the use of an internal combustion engine. His scheme was developed by two Germans, Karl Benz and Gottlieb Daimler. They were followed by the American, Henry Ford, who started the mass production of cars.

BENZ'S FIRST MOTOR CAR

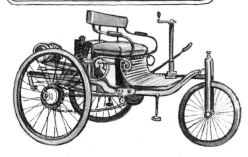

Danger! Slow moving vehicle

Although cars were an interesting invention it was much quicker in the early days to travel by horse or train. This was partly due to the fact that the first cars were not capable of going very fast. In 1878 a law was passed called the 'Red Flag' Act which fixed the maximum speed limit for motor-powered vehicles at 4mph (6½ kph)! The car had to be preceded by a man waving a red flag to warn people on the road of its approach.

GONDOLA

Tarmacadam

The nineteenth century saw a big change in the condition of Britain's roads. The man we have to thank was a Scot called John McAdam who was an investigator of roads. He worked out that instead of using large stones as a base topped with smaller ones, the whole road surface should be made of small, angular stones which packed together for a tight base. No stone which a worker could not fit into his mouth was to be used! This process was named Macadamisation after its inventor and meant that mail coaches could now travel at twice the speed. These improved roads were the best Britain had had since the Romans left 1400 years before! By 1824 London roads were macadamised. In 1882, the system was improved by covering the stones with tar – hence the name tarmacadam – which became shortened to the word we use today, tarmac.

Full steam ahead

With the coming of the railways, areas like the Lake District were opened up to tourists as well as providing cheaper and quicker transport from the copper and slate mines in the hills. In 1860 the Furness Railway Company decided to branch out and launch a new passenger service – an elegant yacht powered by steam to take people on trips round the beautiful lake of Coniston Water. The craft was christened *Gondola* and could carry about ninety people. Tourists enjoyed trips on *Gondola* for seventy-six years but in 1936 she was put into retirement. Forty years on, people decided it was time for her to rise again and sail Coniston. Money was raised and in 1980 *Gondola* was relaunched. If you visit the Lake District make sure you take a trip on this graceful Victorian steam yacht.

Phones, photos and fridges

Can you imagine a life without telephones, recorded music, radio, photographs? Have you ever been in a power cut and felt helpless without electricity? This is what it would have been like if you lived in Britain at the time of the young Queen Victoria. However, by the time Victoria died in 1901 Britain had gramophones, telephones, cameras, washing machines, gas cookers, electric light in houses and on the street and Victoria was the first monarch to have her funeral captured on moving film.

Penny Post

Before 1840 the delivery charges for letters were paid by the person receiving the item rather than the person who had sent it. This was very bad news for poor people who'd moved away from home or gone away overseas in search of work. It could cost as much as a tenth of a week's wages to send a letter from London to Ireland, for example. A reformer called Rowland Hill researched into how much it actually cost to send a letter and worked out that charges were ridiculously high. He suggested having a prepaid fee for sending letters, starting at one penny. In spite of great opposition from the Post Office, who saw that their profits would drop dramatically, he managed to get his scheme accepted and in 1840 the Penny Post started. Twenty-five years later the number of letters and packets being sent by mail had increased ninefold to 642 million.

THE PENNY BLACK THE FIRST POSTAGE STAMP

POSTAGE · ONE PENNY ·

VICTORIAN WALKMAN

MARCONI'S WIRELESS

Codes and telegraph wires

The advance of Morse code and the telegraph system meant that the British Parliament learnt of the death of Tsar Nicholas I of Russia the same day in 1855, whereas seventy-nine years before, in 1776, it had taken seven weeks (by ship) before Britain heard that America had declared itself independent.

Other inventions

- **1837** shorthand was invented by Isaac Pitman and is still in use today
- **Around 1850** the first washing machines came on the market with a rotating drum and mangle
- **1865** the first Singer Family Sewing Machine went on sale. Within twenty years over 4 million homes had one. Paper patterns were printed for easy dressmaking and the way was opened for cheap off-the-peg clothes rather than exclusively hand-tailored garments
- **1876** Alexander Graham Bell invented the telephone
- **1877** Edison invented the gramophone (forerunner of our record player)
- **1896** Marconi demonstrated his wireless radio in Britain

BELL'S TELEPHONE

EDISON'S GRAMOPHONE

RECEIVER

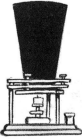

TRANSMITTER

Snap!

If you visit Lacock in Wiltshire you'll be able to see Lacock Abbey, the home of William Henry Fox Talbot, one of the pioneers of photography. Using a 'mousetrap' camera made by a local carpenter, Fox Talbot took the world's first negative in 1835 and made a print of it. You can see his other early experiments in photography at the Fox Talbot Museum in Lacock. The Talbot family were not interested in any development apart from photographic (geddit???) and made sure that during the railway boom no lines were built near Lacock.

FOX TALBOT AND LACOCK ABBEY

Cheese

Cleanliness next to Godliness?

Nineteenth-century Britain was still relatively backward in plumbing. Most country houses made do with a chamber pot, a washstand with a pitcher and bowl, or a hip bath in front of the fire. All the water for washing would have been carried upstairs by servants. However, with the rise of the new rich came new ideas about hygiene: they built their own country houses with all mod cons, and bathrooms began to feature in house design. Some people were slow to adapt – Queen Victoria herself refused to modernise Buckingham Palace after Albert died as she wanted nothing changed; and the Beale family, who built Standen in East Sussex in 1894, chose to have only two bathrooms between twenty-two bedrooms.

Good and bad

Refrigeration meant that fresh foods could be transported longer distances. Earlier, this kind of food only lasted if it had been preserved – that is, salted, pickled or sugared – or kept in an ice house, but once effective refrigeration had been developed, fresh food was available to many more people. In 1880 the first cargo of refrigerated meat arrived from Australia and soon New Zealand and the beef ranches in Argentina also began to supply Britain with cheap meat. The good news was that now poorer people could afford a better diet. But it was bad news for British farmers who couldn't compete with the low prices. Many farmers went out of business and a lot of farm workers lost their jobs and homes.

A modern magician

William Armstrong had two great passions in life: fishing and scientific experiments. He spent so much time fishing that his family called him 'the kingfisher'. As a young man, when he was out fishing, he noticed what efficient use a waterwheel was making of the river's natural power. He became fascinated by water power and in 1847 gave up his job as a solicitor in Newcastle and instead started his own engineering firm, specialising in machines powered by water (hydraulic engineering).

Water on the brain

However, Armstrong's fortune came from designing and manufacturing a new type of gun – no, not water pistols – which he invented after the Crimean War. His Armstrong gun was the forerunner of the modern artillery gun, firing a bullet shell loaded from the back rather than a lead ball shoved down the barrel. The guns were also made of welded steel rather than cast iron and so were much lighter to handle. W.G. Armstrong & Company sold arms to both sides in the American Civil War, and became the second largest arms manufacturer in the world.

Armstrong decided to buy up land near Rothbury in Northumbria to build a holiday home, Cragside. By damming streams he created a series of lakes from where machines pumped water to supply the house with running water as well as powering the central heating, a kitchen spit, an electric sewing machine, a series of electric gongs and laundry equipment.

The servants' friend

Armstrong's lift design was especially useful for the servants who could now use it for carrying heavy scuttles of coal for fires instead of lugging them up endless flights of stairs.

Switched on!

Cragside is most famous for being the first house in the world to be lit by electricity. By harnessing the power from the lakes, Armstrong and his friend Joseph Swan used a water turbine to provide the electricity to light the entire house. This revolutionary system was switched on for the first time in December 1880.

Life downstairs

Even though labour-saving gadgets were coming in to use, every middle-class and upper-class family would still have had at least one servant or maid. In return for a small wage and board and lodging the family had permanent live-in help.

Country houses

Any large country house would have at least eight servants and it was not unusual for some of the largest stately homes to employ over forty indoor staff. Victorian families were often very large which meant that a staff of nannies, governesses, nursemaids and tutors would also be needed. At important dinners there was often one servant to wait on each guest. If guests came to stay they would usually bring their own valet or maid so, as you can imagine, the servants' quarters in a large Victorian house had to be pretty extensive.

A popular job

The 1881 census showed that one in nine of all females over five years of age were indoor servants.

Ding a ling ling

In medieval times the whole household lived together, and servants would sleep outside their employer's door so that they'd be ready to answer any needs. However, by Victorian times a communication system had been developed which meant that the servants could be kept out of the way, and called by bell when necessary.

Servants shouldn't be seen OR heard

Servants were kept invisible as far as possible from the family and guests. Separate staircases were used by staff so they could get about the house without bumping into the family. Some employers took this rule a little far: there are tales of servants having to flatten themselves face to the wall when they saw family or guests coming their way and the Duke of Portland at Welbeck Abbey in Nottinghamshire sacked any housemaid who had the misfortune to meet him in the corridors. Sir Harry Featherstonhaugh of Uppark in West Sussex went to the other extreme – he married his dairymaid in 1825!

Servant segregation

It wasn't only the family that the servants were kept away from – they were also kept away from one another! Menservants lived and slept in different areas from the maids and there were even cases of separate men's and women's staircases. At Lanhydrock in Cornwall there are separate staircases for adults and children, servants and family, as well as men and women servants. One problem area was the laundry's bleaching lawn where sheets were hung out to whiten – this provided an outside meeting place for laundrymaids and amorous stablehands. One employer got over this by building a tunnel for the laundrymaids to use on their way to the drying ground to avoid walking past the stables!

KITCHEN, LANHYDROCK

LAUNDRY, BENINGBROUGH

A large retinue

A large country house would have a housekeeper, butler, cook and kitchen staff, maids and footmen. The staff were divided into 'lower' and 'upper' servants depending on their status. All the rooms in the servants' wing had separate functions: in addition to the pantry, larders and stores connected with the running of the kitchen, there might be a bakery, a brewery, a knife room, a lamp room, shoe room and brushing room. The laundry was a highly organised separate area, with wash house, drying room, mangling room, ironing room, folding room and laundrymaids' room arranged so that dirty clothes went in at one end and clean clothes came out the other. You can see a Victorian laundry at Beningbrough Hall in North Yorkshire and Castle Ward, Northern Ireland.

'Downstairs' to visit:

Dunham Massey, Cheshire

Lyme Park, Cheshire

Lanhydrock, Cornwall

Calke Abbey, Derbyshire

Penrhyn Castle, Gwynedd

Erddig, Clwyd

Charlecote Park, Warwickshire

Speke Hall, Merseyside

Tatton Park, Cheshire

Shugborough, Staffordshire

Castle Ward, Northern Ireland

Florence Court, Northern Ireland

EDWARD BARNES, WOODMAN, ERDDIG, 1830

Victorian attitudes

The technological developments and booming industry of Victorian Britain meant that more people could earn a good salary and imitate the upper classes. This new middle class set up small businesses and entered professional careers like teaching, law, medicine, banking or shopkeeping. They liked to think they had very respectable lives: they went to church, dressed smartly, disapproved of drinking and brought up their children to be 'seen and not heard'. Middle-class families tended to live in towns and cities, in large terrace houses with maybe one or two servants.

CHURCH, CLUMBER PARK

COTTAGE, BLAISE HAMLET

Pious people

Although we think of the Victorian age as a very moral and religious time, a census in 1851 showed that only one in three people regularly went to church. Prince Albert's moral influence changed this and soon people were becoming more religious and some landowners commissioned large new churches to be built on their land to show the strength of their faith. You can see late Victorian churches at Studley Royal in Yorkshire and Clumber Park in Nottinghamshire.

Bad attendance ...

When Victoria stayed at Wimpole Hall in Cambridgeshire in 1873 she got up to go to morning prayers and found that the only other people in the chapel were the servants. The family were still in bed.

Helping the poor

Much of the population lived in miserable poverty during Victorian times. But there were groups and individuals who tried to help the worse off. The Quakers, a Christian group, did their bit by being good employers. Many Quaker families like the Frys, Cadburys and Rowntrees went into the chocolate business in the late 1840s because they saw it as a way of improving the diet of the poor. Another Quaker, a banker called John Harford, owned the Blaise Castle estate near Bristol. In 1810 he commissioned a top architect of the day, John Nash, to build a collection of picturesque thatched cottages to house retired workers from the estate. The model village was named Blaise Hamlet and you can still visit it today. Another good employer was Sir Thomas Acland of Killerton in Devon. He made sure all his servants, estate workers and farm tenants had decent housing, schooling and health care.

Adam or Ape?

In 1859 Charles Darwin published a book called *The Origin of Species* which explained the theory that man had evolved from an ape and was not – as the Bible taught – descended from Adam and Eve. This was a huge shock to most Victorians who took the Bible literally and many thought Darwin was off his head and a blasphemer.

Fashionable puffing

Smoking, like church-going, was another habit which grew popular again in the nineteenth century. This was partly because the Prince Consort and the Prince of Wales both smoked. Not everyone agreed with the new fashion – the Duke of Wellington made guests smoke in the servants' hall at Stratfield Saye and Sir John Boileau of Ketteringham in Norfolk never invited back guests whom he found smoking. However, houses began to include special rooms for smoking where the men could go after dinner, wearing smoking jackets, sit in a haze of blue smoke, talk about male subjects and maybe play a game of billiards. You can see Victorian billiard rooms at Dunster Castle in Somerset and Knightshayes Court in Devon.

BILLIARD ROOM, CRAGSIDE

Dry houses

Many Victorians took a very dim view of drinking and saw it as a cause of ruin of many families. Leaflets were printed warning of the evils of drink and several 'teetotal' or abstinence groups were formed, including the Blue Ribbon Army whose members wore a blue ribbon on their jackets. Sir Walter Calverley Trevelyan who lived at Wallington in Northumberland believed strongly in teetotalism and there were no pubs in the estate village, Cambo. When his father died in 1846 one of the first things Sir Walter did was to empty all the bottles from his father's enormous wine cellar into the lake at the family home in Somerset.

Riding restrictions

Women had quite a restricted time. Even when they went out riding they had to ride side-saddle, wearing layers and layers of petticoats and even trousers underneath their dress in case they fell off and revealed any bare flesh! If they did fall, many women would end up hanging upside down from the saddle, caught up in their petticoats. Thankfully in 1880 someone had the bright idea of inventing the divided skirt and women could ride normally.

Take cover!

Even at the fashionable seaside resorts people were very careful about revealing too much. The severest bathing suits covered people from top to toe and changing huts were wheeled out to sea so that people could sink into the water without being seen in their bathing suit.

Stretching a point!

The Victorian feelings for modesty even went as far as table and piano legs which they covered up in case they offended anyone!

Health and hygiene

Early Victorian towns and cities were fairly unpleasant places with open sewers, polluted water supplies, dirty streets and crowded living conditions. They were the perfect breeding ground for diseases like cholera, tuberculosis, typhoid and typhus and death rates were high. In 1875 town councils were made responsible for drainage, sewage, street cleaning and the supply of fresh water so gradually diseases carried by water – like cholera – were reduced.

Falling disease ... rising families

As research into medicine improved and the sanitary conditions in towns became better, the death rate fell and so more children survived childhood. As a result it was not unusual for families to have ten or twelve children.

Kill or cure?

Although medicine was developing rapidly, treatment was still pretty basic for the first half of Victoria's reign. People dreaded getting ill. Surgery was particularly hit and miss, and didn't seem to have advanced much since the Middle Ages. Red hot irons were used to clean wounds and ulcers but surgical instruments were not sterilised so gangrene and poisoning often set in as a result of an operation. Blood-sucking leeches were still regarded as a good way of getting rid of nasty substances from the body.

Grateful mothers

Queen Victoria was delighted when chloroform was brought in as an effective and safe pain killer. She used it when she gave birth to her eighth child, Leopold. Another mother was so overcome and delighted with her relatively painless childbirth that she called her daughter Anaesthesia!

Improvements

Things were definitely getting better by the end of the century: doctors had begun to inject people against cholera and typhoid; X-rays had been discovered in 1895 by a German scientist; and, in France, Marie and Pierre Curie's experiments found that radium could be used to treat cancer. Another headache went in 1899 with the invention of aspirin.

Wholesome food

In the latter part of the century, laws were introduced to stop corrupt suppliers adding substances to food to increase their profit. A favourite trick was to water down milk or add plaster of Paris to flour. Substitute foods like evaporated milk and margarine were produced to get round the problem, but they did not have so much nutritional value.

CLAYDON HOUSE

Florence Nightingale

The lady of the lamp

In 1854-6 Britain and France went to war in the Crimea to help the Turks fight against Russia. Britain hadn't been to war since 1815 and there was a lack of good leadership in the army. Many soldiers lost their lives. However, it was the first war when journalists were allowed to send back eye-witness reports. Because of this, the public in Britain soon got to hear of the dreadful conditions in which the soldiers were living.

One of the worst things to come to light was that care for the wounded was practically non-existent and so the death rate from injuries was horribly high. Florence Nightingale, a 35-year-old lady from a wealthy family, who'd been doing some research into nursing in England, offered to go out with a team of nurses and help the wounded. By forcing modern hospital management on the army authorities and insisting on basic standards of hygiene she and her nurses managed to reduce the death rate. She became known as 'the Lady of the Lamp' for her night patrols around the wards. When she returned to England she founded the first training school for nurses at St Thomas's Hospital in London. Other hospitals followed her lead and by 1900 there were 64,000 trained nurses in Britain.

Florence's sister, Parthenope, had married Sir Harry Verney and lived at Claydon House in Buckinghamshire. If you go there you can read various letters which Florence wrote from the Crimea, describing the awful conditions there.

The British abroad

The British Empire reached its greatest size in the nineteenth century. The lands Britain ruled included Canada, India, Australia and New Zealand, parts of Africa and the Far East as well as many Caribbean, Pacific and Indian Ocean islands. The Empire was a great source of wealth for British industry. Bradford, Leeds and Manchester became major textile centres as a consequence of the raw cotton which came in from various parts of the Empire. The clothes made from these materials were then sold to other countries for a profit. Other valuable items which came from colonies were grain, meat and timber.

Scramble

In the 1870s European countries began to get greedy for land overseas. They concentrated their efforts on founding colonies in Africa. With the developments in firearms and medicine, Europeans were more confident about exploring the interior and this rush to claim land became known as 'the Scramble for Africa'.

The Indian Mutiny

India was a country rich in silk, cotton and tea. From the 1600s until 1858 much of India was ruled by a British organisation called the East India Company, which also controlled the trade between England and India. In 1857 Muslim and Hindu Indian troops of the British army revolted because they had been forced to use bullets which had been greased with pig fat – an unclean animal to Muslims, and beef fat – the holy animal of the Hindus. After the mutiny had been defeated, the British Government appointed a Viceroy, a man acting as a deputy for the monarch, to govern India. Lord Curzon of Kedleston Hall in Derbyshire was Viceroy of India for six years from 1899. If you visit Kedleston you will see many objects he bought back from India in a special museum in the house.

Gold rush!

Australia had been a convenient place for Britain to ship her convicts since the late eighteenth century. However, in 1851 gold was discovered and thousands of people left Britain to make their fortunes the other side of the world. Between 1850 and 1860 the population of Australia increased sevenfold.

Native Australians, the Aborigines, suffered with the coming of the white man. Many became infected or died from diseases brought over from Europe. They were a nomadic people who gradually found their lands being taken up and enclosed by the settlers, destroying their natural way of life.

New Zealand

In the early part of the nineteenth century, trade with New Zealand had been limited to adventurous Europeans setting up trading posts dealing in a few goods including preserved Maori heads. However, in 1840 Maori chiefs signed the Treaty of Waitangi with British settlers, bringing New Zealand into the Empire.

The Boer War

The Boers, descendants of the Dutch, were the main white population of the Cape Colony in South Africa. But in 1806 Britain took over the governing of this area. The Boers were unhappy with the change and between 1835 and 1842 around 12,000 left and travelled north to set up their own Boer Republic. Later in the century gold and diamonds were discovered here and many Britons moved in to work the mines – but they quarrelled with the Boers over political rights. In 1899 a bitter war broke out between Britain and the Boers which lasted for three years. The Boers were outnumbered by five to one but had the advantage of knowing the country and fought a very effective guerrilla war until the British commander Lord Kitchener decided to take drastic measures. He rounded up the Boers and put them into concentration camps and burnt their farms. Over 20,000 died in the camps and the Boer fighters were forced to admit defeat in 1902.

Reginald Pole-Carew of Antony House in Cornwall fought in the Boer War and was knighted on his return.

Down under in Surrey

If you visit Clandon Park in Surrey you'll find an unlikely building in the garden. It is a Maori meeting house brought back by the 4th Earl of Onslow who was Governor of New Zealand from 1888 to 1892 – it is one of the oldest in existence. His son was presented with a Maori chieftain's cloak of kiwi feathers as a christening present and given the honorary Maori name of Huia.

LORD
KITCHENER

A long way from home

With the overcrowding in towns and cities people were encouraged to emigrate. Most people ended up going to either Canada, Australia, New Zealand or the USA. This would have been a traumatic decision, involving a long and dangerous sea journey to a strange land. Emigrants would probably never see family and friends who they left behind again. Often there was little choice: in the 1840s Ireland suffered a terrible famine and over 1.5 million people left the country to escape starvation.

MAORI HUT, CLANDON PARK

A grim life

As industrial sites grew up in cities, people began to move away from the countryside to find new jobs in the factories. The pay was better than farm labouring and there was more work available. Cities filled to bursting point – London was particularly badly affected: in 1801 the capital housed 16.9 per cent of Britain's population but only fifty years later 50 per cent of the country lived there. Most cities were not prepared for the sudden increase in population and people lived in terrible conditions. Streets were infested with rats, sewers could not cope and disease ran riot.

Factory owners often put up cheap houses for workers. These back-to-backs were badly built with just two rooms: a living room on the ground floor and bedroom above. There was no water, no back yard and whole streets would share only a few privies.

BACK TO BACK HOUSES

Not all bad

Some industrialists were more caring and thought that people would work better if they had decent places to live. The Lever brothers who ran a soapmaking factory in Lancashire built a village for their workers called Port Sunlight and gave them medical care and a share of the profits.

St John's Institute

The East End of London was originally a pleasant area to live for workers in the city. But it got swallowed up by industrial developments and anyone who could afford to, moved out. For those who were left, life could be grim. Some people tried to make things a bit better for the people living in these areas. In 1890 the rector of St John-at-Hackney bought Sutton House, a large building dating back to the early sixteenth century. He converted it into a St John's Institute, a recreation centre for working men. If you visit Sutton House you will see old photographs showing the building when it was an institute.

Crime and punishment

With overcrowding and poverty in cities the crime rate soared. People who were caught were punished severely – the worst offenders were sent to Australia or hanged. Stealing got a more serious sentence than violence and murder. After 1840 criminals were no longer sent to Australia but were kept in British prisons where conditions were awful, with almost no sanitation and very little food. Towards the end of the century, attitudes began to change and people started to realise that prisons should be reforming institutions rather than punishing houses.

SUTTON HOUSE

Local bobby

The first policemen in London were known as the Bow Street Runners. After 1829 they wore uniforms and were known as Peelers or Bobbies, after their founder Robert Peel, the Prime Minister of the day. In 1856 the County and Borough Police Act was passed making it compulsory for every county in Britain to have a permanent police force.

Famous Victorians Wordsearch
Find these ten famous people

KINGSLEY
NIGHTINGALE
VICTORIA
BERTIE
ALBERT
DISRAELI
GLADSTONE
KITCHENER
ARMSTRONG
HILL

Answers on page 32

```
R A V O L T S H E E G T
E R U I T B E R N B T L
N M X D C W Y O I Z I B
E S G I Q T T L G J E E
H T T S U S O A H R C N
C R F R D A I R T S O V
T O Y A E T P I I C A T
I N L E M B E D N A P I
K G Z L Y E L S G N I K
S T H I L L N A A B R O
R J N P K C I K L C E D
L A R T P S K U E V S G
```

Hard times

Charles Dickens, the famous Victorian novelist, based many of his books on the horrors of city life, including *Hard Times* which he wrote in 1854. By 1875 conditions in towns had become so bad that the government decided it was time to take action. The Artisans Dwelling Act was passed which allowed councils to demolish slums and provide better housing.

Charles Dickens

OCTAVIA HILL

CANON RAWNSLEY

From little acorns great oak trees grow ....

Many middle- and upper-class Victorians were horrified at the way the poor were forced to live in cities. One of these was Octavia Hill who became a great housing reformer. She bought up bad housing and used the money from rent to improve it. She had spent her childhood living in the country and one of her key ideas was that people in cities should have access to open spaces like commons and parks for fresher air and exercise. She was also concerned that built-up areas shouldn't spread and gobble up the surrounding countryside.

In 1895, with two other like-minded people – Canon Hardwicke Rawnsley and Robert Hunter – she formed an organisation called The National Trust for Places of Historic Interest or Natural Beauty to preserve land and buildings in danger of development. The National Trust has come a long way since the early days and now owns and protects over 569,000 acres (230,000 hectares) of land and coastline as well as hundreds of historic houses.

Houses and gardens

Garden fashion

In the eighteenth century it had been the fashion to make gardens more like parks with 'natural landscaping'. This meant that flower beds and 'fussy' planting schemes were grassed over in favour of large areas of lawn which merged into the parkland. However, during the nineteenth century plant collectors, travelling to all corners of the world, brought back interesting plant specimens to England. The old-fashioned flower garden came back into favour again, but now there were many more varieties of plant with which to experiment.

GARDEN, BIDDULPH GRANGE

A world of his own

One of the most interesting of Victorian gardens is Biddulph Grange in Staffordshire. It was the idea of James Bateman, a fanatical plant collector who created a mystery garden with plants from all over the world. The garden was divided into areas which conjured up images of different countries: Egypt, China and America just to name a few.

French grandeur

In the 1870s a very unusual, grand house was built in Buckinghamshire by Baron Ferdinand de Rothschild. He was a member of the very influential Frankfurt banking family and had made his home in England. He loved France and so with his enormous wealth built his English country house, Waddesdon, to look like a French chateau. He even went as far as importing French horses to drag the building materials to the hill-top site! Queen Victoria visited Waddesdon in 1890 and planted a tree in the park – the silver spade which she used is still kept in the house.

Homely Standen

In contrast to Waddesdon, Standen in Sussex was built with local materials for the Beale family. They simply wanted a country holiday home. The house, built in the 1890s, had to have room for a family of nine and a few servants but didn't need grand rooms for entertaining. It was designed by Philip Webb, an architect who liked his houses to be plainly built with high quality materials and to have comfortable interiors.

STANDEN

WADDESDON

Arts and Crafts

Philip Webb was a friend and associate of William Morris, the well-known designer who founded a firm of interior decorators in 1861. Morris was a designer with a difference -- he had been very worried about the falling standards of craftsmanship and design since the industrial revolution and set up his firm to promote well-made products NOT mass-produced goods. His aim was to get back to the same standards of craftsmanship as those of the Middle Ages and with various associates produced furniture, textiles, wallpaper, pottery, jewellery, metalwork and hand-printed books. Morris's ideas inspired the Arts and Crafts Movement which grew in popularity throughout the century and William Morris textiles and decoration appeared in many fashionable houses. William Morris patterns are still very popular today: your house might even have curtains or furnishing based on his designs.

Arts and Crafts houses to visit:

Lindisfarne Castle, Northumberland

Standen, West Sussex

Wightwick Manor, West Midlands

The Arts and Crafts movement also influenced garden design with several owners returning to simple, cottage-style gardens using old-fashioned plants.

Arts and Crafts gardens to visit:

Ightham Mote, Kent

Snowshill Manor, Gloucestershire

Wightwick Manor, West Midlands

Standen, West Sussex

William Morris

Houses for new men

Many successful businessmen who had done well in industry built grand houses with their new wealth. Penrhyn Castle in Gwynedd was built to look like a Norman castle for the Pennant family who owned an extremely profitable slate quarry. Wightwick Manor in the West Midlands was built by Theodore Mander, a paint manufacturer from Wolverhampton. Many other established families extended and modernised their stately homes in this era of change.

KITCHEN, LINDISFARNE CASTLE

Kitchen planning

Food in Victorian times was cooked on ranges heated by coal. Large houses had extra stoves and stewing pans for heating up more pots or keeping food warm. As there were no proper ventilation systems, kitchen smells were very strong. There was a difficult choice to make: you either kept the kitchen close to the dining-room and had hot food but smells or you put the kitchen out on a limb, giving no smells but cold food. People usually went for the cold food option but would have a hotplate in the serving room next to the dining-room to warm the food up after its long trip.

Just for fun

Crooked croquet

Croquet was a popular Victorian sport, especially for women, who found they could still play even in their restricting clothing. In fact, ladies wearing crinolines had an advantage as they could sneakily move the ball to a better position using their skirts!

A good deal

In 1861 a man called Thomas Cook organised the first mass package holiday. He sent 1,700 working class holiday makers from London to Paris and back with five nights accommodation (choice of 13 hotels) and all meals for 46 shillings (£2.30) per person. Other popular holiday spots were spa towns and the seaside. Thomas Cook's travel business is still going strong 130 years later.

Football fever

The first F A Cup competition was held in 1871. Today's famous football teams started off as church, chapel, school or factory sides. Manchester United was made up of men who worked for the Lancashire and Yorkshire Railway Company, while Arsenal's team was originally a group of workers making guns at the Woolwich Arsenal (which explains why they're nicknamed 'The Gunners').

Anyone for tennis?

In 1837 Major Walter Wingfield invented a game called 'Sphairistike' – a forerunner of lawn tennis. In the next few years a set of standardised rules was issued and the name was changed to lawn tennis (which is a lot easier to say!). The All England Croquet Club, based in Wimbledon, decided to give over one of its bowling lawns to the new sport, and the first Lawn Tennis Championship was held there in 1877.

Holiday time

Before 1871 people did not get paid holidays and many worked year in, year out without a break. The only exceptions were Sundays, Christmas Day and Good Friday and occasionally Saturday afternoon. But from 1871 banks were also allowed to close on Easter Monday, Whit Monday, the first Monday in August and Boxing Day. These 'bank holidays' soon became public holidays because little business could take place without banks.

Cricket championship

Cricket has been a popular sport since the eighteenth century: the famous Marylebone Cricket Club (MCC) was formed by a group of noblemen in 1787. The Club started the County Championship in 1873, but only nine counties qualified then, and Gloucestershire dominated the field thanks to the legendary cricketer, W.G. Grace and his two brothers.

The Dancing Marquess

Some took theatricals VERY seriously. The 5th Marquess of Anglesey, who inherited Plas Newydd in North Wales in 1898, was an extremely exotic character. He loved dressing up in elaborate costumes, ran a private theatre at Plas Newydd and also took his touring theatrical company all over Europe. All his productions were hideously expensive and this, together with a passion for buying clothes and jewels, meant that the Dancing Marquess went bankrupt in 1904. It took three days of auctioning to sell the contents of his wardrobe!

Long winter evenings

In these days before television, videos and cinema, people had to make their own entertainment. Famous authors like Charles Dickens and the Brontës had their works serialised in magazines, and each week readers waited impatiently to find out what happened next to Oliver Twist or Jane Eyre. Most well-to-do families would have a piano and sometimes evenings would be spent gathered round singing songs. The McGeogh family at The Argory in Northern Ireland went one step further and commissioned a special organ to be built for their house.

Amateur dramatics was another way of passing the time. At Wimpole Hall in Cambridgeshire the Gallery was converted into a makeshift theatre with curtains hung between the columned screen and plays were performed and often written by members of the family. In the professional theatre, audiences flocked to see Edmund Keane, Sir Henry Irving and Ellen Terry. You can visit Ellen Terry's home, Smallhythe Place in Kent, and see theatrical mementoes of this period.

On your bike!

The bicycle went through several stages of development during the nineteenth century. Before 1817 steering had not been perfected, and many people thought they were extremely dangerous. Some said that it was easier to avoid a mad dog than a madman on a bicycle because at least the dog ran in a straight line! Until rubber tyres were invented in 1890 people rode on bare steel or wooden tyres – no wonder the early bicycles were called 'boneshakers'. Probably the best-known early design of bicycle was the penny-farthing, designed by James Starley in 1870. His aim was to make a lighter machine than the heavy-framed boneshaker bicycles. The large front wheel with the smaller stabilising back wheel gave the bike its nickname – penny-farthing – after the smallest and largest coins of the day. Bicycles, especially the penny-farthing, became extremely popular. They were cheaper than public transport and were four times as fast as walking and twice as fast as a horse and carriage.

If you visit Snowshill in Gloucestershire you can see Charles Wade's collection of boneshaker bicycles in the room of One Hundred Wheels.

Rich kids

The children of rich Victorian families would have had nannies to look after them and governesses to teach them in their early years. Their childhood would have been spent in the nursery wing of the house and many only saw their parents once a day when they had to be on best behaviour. They would eat separately from their parents and were taught to leave clean plates – if they didn't, the left-over food would be served up again at the next meal!

Terrible tales

Life for the Victorian child was often not much fun. Children were meant to be 'seen not heard' and much of the time in the nursery was spent playing with educational toys and reading books which usually had very moral stories. One of the most popular books of the day was a translation of a German book called 'Struwwelpeter' which told horrible stories of nasty things that happened to 'bad' children. One of the worst tells of a boy who has both his thumbs cut off because he wouldn't give up sucking his thumb ...

Unisex clothes

Until boys were four or five they wore dresses like girls. If you look at portraits of young children it's often difficult to tell whether it's a boy or girl. Queen Victoria influenced the fashion for British children quite by chance. She ordered a miniature sailor suit to be made for Bertie, the Prince of Wales, when he was five. Soon this style of dress was THE thing for small boys and girls to wear. Victoria also started the craze for tartan with her love of Scotland and kilts were a popular choice for children.

Different for girls

Although they were dressed the same when small children, boys and girls of middle- and upper-class families were soon treated very differently. The main aim for daughters was to get them married: they were taught all the things which would make an attractive bride – to play the piano, sew, paint, sing, stand properly and make polite conversation. Girls were usually taught at home by a governess, and educational subjects were often limited to scripture, French and German.

Bullied boys

The sons of wealthy parents were sent away to boarding public schools like Rugby, Eton, Harrow and Winchester. These schools were known more for their bullying than education and some boys had a miserable time. The book *Tom Brown's Schooldays* exposed the bullying that went on at Rugby.

Sons from the middle class would go to grammar schools, usually day schools and a lot cheaper than public schools. Some of these schools had been founded in the fifteenth and sixteenth centuries and their main aim was to teach Latin and Greek grammar.

Nurseries to visit:
Erddig, North Wales
Wightwick Manor, West Midlands
Castle Ward, Northern Ireland
Berrington Hall, Hereford & Worcester
Nunnington Hall, North Yorkshire
Springhill, Northern Ireland

Collections of toys:
Snowshill, Gloucestershire
Sudbury Museum of Childhood, Derbyshire
Arlington Court, Devon

Poor kids

Poor children in Victorian times suffered terrible hardships despite efforts by reformers to improve matters. The main problem was that children could be sent to work almost as soon as they could walk and many were used as cheap labour in mines and factories.

Sooty and sweep

Small boys would be driven up chimneys to clean out the soot. The chimneys were usually very narrow and twisted, and masters found it more efficient to use small boys rather than a long brush. Children often got stuck or froze with terror in the cramped, darkness – in these cases the master would simply light the fire underneath to 'encourage' them to get on with their work. Because of the soot, chimney boys ended up with breathing problems, while climbing round the nooks and crannies meant that their young, growing bones became crooked. At Sudbury Museum of Childhood in Derbyshire you can climb up inside a chimney yourself (as long as you're aged seven or younger).

In 1863 Charles Kingsley wrote a book called *The Water Babies*. It tells the tale of a young sweep, Tom, who drowns while trying to escape from his evil master and comes back to life underwater as a 'water baby'. Malham Tarn in Yorkshire is supposed to be where Kingsley imagined Tom lived his life as a water baby. Lord Shaftesbury, a fierce opponent of child labour, took up the cause of the chimney-sweep boys and through his campaigning an act was passed in 1864 making it illegal for boys to be used as sweeps.

Slavery at home

When slavery was abolished in the British Empire in 1833 many made the point that lots of people in Britain were working in conditions which were almost as bad. In 1842, women and children were forbidden to work underground in mines, and five years later an act was passed saying that women and children should not work for more than ten hours a day.

APPRENTICE HOUSE, STYAL.

Children at work

If you want to see what life was like for children working in a factory mill, you can visit Quarry Bank Mill at Styal, Cheshire (pictured on the front cover). This cotton mill, built by the Greg family in 1784, employed ninety children or 'apprentices' to work in the factory; they made up a third of the workforce. The children were sometimes orphans who were handed over by parish authorities anxious to get rid of the responsibility of looking after them. But even parents would sign away their children to the scheme. In return for taking the children on, housing and feeding them and giving them a basic education, the mill got a very cheap resident labour force. The children lived together in the Apprentice House, slept two to a bed and worked for twelve or thirteen hours a day, six days a week. Although there is no evidence that child workers at Styal were badly treated, it would have been a very hard life and many of the jobs working with the mill machinery were dangerous.

If you visit Quarry Bank Mill you can see the largest working waterwheel in the country. The demonstrations and displays give the feeling of what the nineteenth-century factory was like.

Education for all?

Working class children hardly ever got the chance to go to school because they were sent to work or had to look after younger brothers and sisters while their parents went out to work.

Schools available for the poor varied. There were some charity schools like the Blewcoat School in Victoria, London, which dates from 1709, or else there were schools at workhouses, factory schools or Sunday schools at church. Children would have used slates to write on and learnt how to read, write and work out basic maths. From 1870 all children between five and ten were supposed to be educated and so new schools were needed. Children at these new Board schools had to pay a few pence and many parents couldn't even afford this small sum.

The Blewcoat School.

A reformer

One of the main educational reformers of the nineteenth century was Dr James Kay. In 1839 he became the secretary of a new government education committee that made many important improvements. He later married a member of the Shuttleworth family who lived at Gawthorpe Hall in Lancashire and became Sir James Kay-Shuttleworth.

A change for the worse

Although Board schools were made free for everyone in 1891, parents still were reluctant to send their children because they didn't want to lose the income from their earnings. Factory owners were also against education as they didn't want to have to pay more for adults to do the children's jobs; the younger the child was, the less the factory owner had to pay. As a result, some children ended up with a terrible deal: a half-time system was introduced which meant that children would work for a few hours in the factory before school started and then go back after school and work until ten o'clock at night. This system wasn't abolished until 1918 when the minimum age for children working in factories was raised to twelve.

Make a kaleidoscope

The Victorians were fascinated by kaleidoscopes and it's easy to make a simple one. All you need is 150mm (6") of mirror board from a craft shop – or a smooth sheet of silver foil glued on to some stiff card.

1. Mark the plain side of the card with a pencil, dividing it into three equal rectangles.

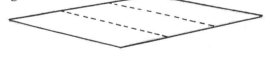

2. Score lightly along the lines with a pair of scissors (but do not cut).

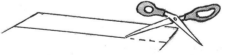

3. Fold the board into a triangular tube with the mirror on the inside and secure with tape.

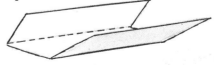

4. Look through the tube at different coloured objects and shapes around you. Turn it and watch the changing patterns in the mirrors.

Victorian women

Nearly everything about the Victorian woman's life was restricting, including her clothes. Because it was fashionable to have wasp-like waists, women poured themselves into whalebone corsets which were sometimes laced up so tightly that they fainted. Until 1870 the fashion for women was to wear crinolines – huge, wide skirts over a series of bamboo hoops – which may have looked impressive but were very impractical. After 1870 the bustle became popular and wasn't quite such a hindrance to movement. You can see many Victorian costumes on display at Killerton in Devon.

Marriage trap

In early Victorian times women had few legal rights. When a woman married, everything she owned became her husband's. Even if she happened to work, the money she earned was his too. It was almost impossible for a woman to divorce her husband – this had to be agreed by Parliament until 1857, and was only possible if there was proof that husband or wife had committed adultery.

Life for unmarried women could be even worse, especially if they had no training of any sort. Spinsters would live at home with elderly parents filling in the time doing needlework and watercolour painting.

The angel in the house

Hardly any upper-class women worked. They had nannies to look after children and servants to run the house, leaving them free to be dutiful and obedient wives.

Career planning

In the second half of the nineteenth century there were more job opportunities for women. In 1848 women were allowed to go to London University, while Oxford's Lady Margaret Hall and Cambridge's Newnham College for women were both founded in the 1870s. Nearly all women graduates looking for a job became teachers and after 1870, when education was compulsory, there were many vacancies. Until the invention of the telephone and telegraph, the only jobs for most lower-class women were as a domestic servant. Now they could get better jobs in the new companies as switchboard operators.

Doctors and nurses

Nursing had also become a respectable profession thanks to Florence Nightingale and in 1876 women could be admitted to medical schools to train as doctors. The first British woman doctor, Elizabeth Garrett, qualified in 1870 but met with great opposition from her male student colleagues. Many women patients felt much happier with women doctors – because of Victorian modesty many women would not get undressed for medical examinations by male doctors and often serious illnesses remained undetected as a result.

Emancipation!

A number of women managed to make their mark despite the restrictions of Victorian society. Elizabeth Garrett's sister Agnes, and her cousin Rhoda, set up their own interior design company after Rhoda had completed her training as an architect – totally unheard of for a woman! Some of their furniture can be seen at Standen in West Sussex.

Although some improvements were made, women were still not allowed to vote in elections. Only in 1884 were all men given the right to vote. In 1897 groups known as suffragettes started pressurising the government to give women the vote. They took quite drastic action to get attention, such as chaining themselves to railings and holding huge demonstrations in London. Not all women wanted the vote or approved of the suffragettes. Queen Victoria described the campaign as a 'mad, wicked, folly'. It took until 1918 for the Government to give the vote to women over thirty – ten years later the voting age was lowered to twenty-one.

Answers

Page 23
Famous Victorians Wordsearch

```
R A V O L T S H E E G T
E R U I T B E R N B T L
N M X D C W Y O I Z I B
E S G I Q T T L G J E E
H T T S U S O A H R C N
C R F R D A I R T S O V
T O Y A E T P I I C A T
I N L E M B E D N A P I
K G Z L Y E L S G N I K
S T H I L L N A A B R O
R J N P K C I K L C E D
L A R T P S K U E V S G
```

Page 9 Activity Box

A. 3   B. 1   C. 4   D. 2

First published in 1993 by National Trust (Enterprises) Ltd, 36 Queen Anne's Gate, London SW1H 9AS Registered Charity No. 205846

ISBN   0 7078 0167 2

Designed by Blade Communications, Leamington Spa
Printed in England

FRONT COVER: Quarry Bank Mill, Styal, Cheshire. This cotton mill is now powered by water: the waterwheel was restored to working order in 1992. The mill is owned by the National Trust but administered by Quarry Bank Mill Trust.